LIFE IS BEAUTIFUL

The start of each day is a promise of love.

Do small things with great love.

Life is hard by the yard; by the inch, it's a cinch.

Let your faith be bigger than your fear.

Love never fails.
— I Corinthians 13:8

Live. Laugh. Love.

Dream big dreams.

Love bears all things, believes all things,
hopes all things, endures all things.

Enjoy the little things.

Little by little does the trick.

— Aesop

Plant your feet firmly but let your heart have wings.

ACT AS
THOUGH IT
WERE
IMPOSSIBLE
TO FAIL.

— Ralph Waldo Emerson

There is only one happiness in life,
to love and be loved.
— George Sand

When life gives you lemons, make margaritas.

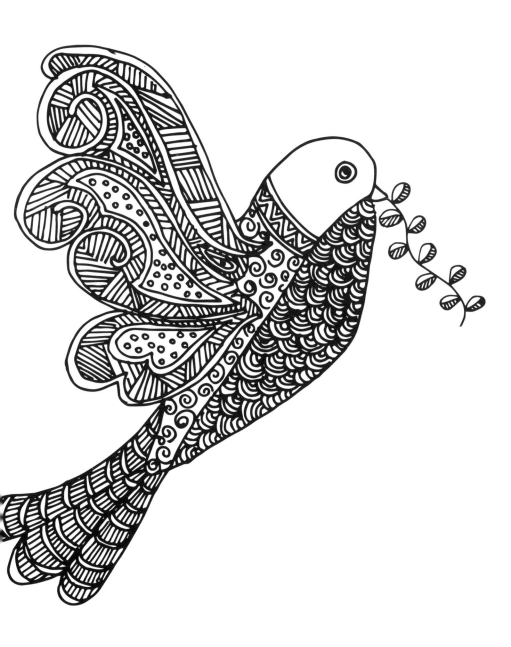

Don't wait for your ship
to come in. Swim out to it.

Life isn't about waiting for the storm to pass;
it's about learning to dance in the rain.

I praise you because I am fearfully and wonderfully made.

— Psalm 139:14

So now faith, hope and love abide . . .
but the greatest of these is love.
— I Corinthians 13:13

Blessed are the happiness makers.

Hope steadies the faltering soul

Little things mean a lot.

Be your own kind of beautiful.

Make your own dream
into reality.

Gratitude is the sign of noble souls.

- Aesop

_____

_____

_____

_____

_____

_____

_____

_____

_____

_____

_____

_____

_____

_____

_____

_____

_____

_____

The heart that loves is always young.
— Greek proverb

The world is but a canvas to our imaginations.
— Henry David Thoreau

Flexible people don't get bent out of shape.

The time to be happy is now. The place to be happy is here.

Do what you love. Love what you do.

It is better to fail in originality than to succeed in imitation.
— Herman Melville

The secret to having it all is believing that you already do.

It is never the wrong time to do the right thing.

Home is where the heart is.

The world is but a school of inquiry.
— Michel de Montaign

THIS is my happy place.

You don't have a soul. You have a body. You are a soul.

If nothing ever changed, there would be no butterflies.

Hope is putting faith to work when doubting would be easier.

○○○○ ————————————————

Whatever you are, be a good one.
— Abraham Lincoln

I'm not telling you it's going to be easy.
I'm telling you it's going to be worth it.

All life is an experiment.
The more experiments
you make the better.

— Ralph Waldo Emerson

Attitude is the mind's paintbrush.
It can color any situation.

The best things in life aren't things.

You are my sunshine.

_____

_____

_____

_____

_____

_____

_____

_____

_____

_____

_____

_____

_____

_____

_____

_____

_____

_____

_____

_____

Each of us is here to make sure
that all of us get there.

Personality can open doors, but
character gives you your own key.

The sun does not shine for a few
trees and flowers, but for
the wide world's joy.
— Henry Ward Beecher

T.I.M.E. is the mission statement:
Teach, Inspire, Motivate, and Encourage.

No one can make you feel inferior without your consent.
— Eleanor Roosevelt

In youth we learn; in age we understand.
— Marie Ebner-Eschenbach

Outside show is a poor
substitute for inner worth.
— Aesop

Wake up every morning with the thought that something wonderful is about to happen.

You must do the thing you think you cannot do.
— Eleanor Roosevelt